A LIFE-SIZE guide
to the animal kingdom

# HOW BIG IS THAT?

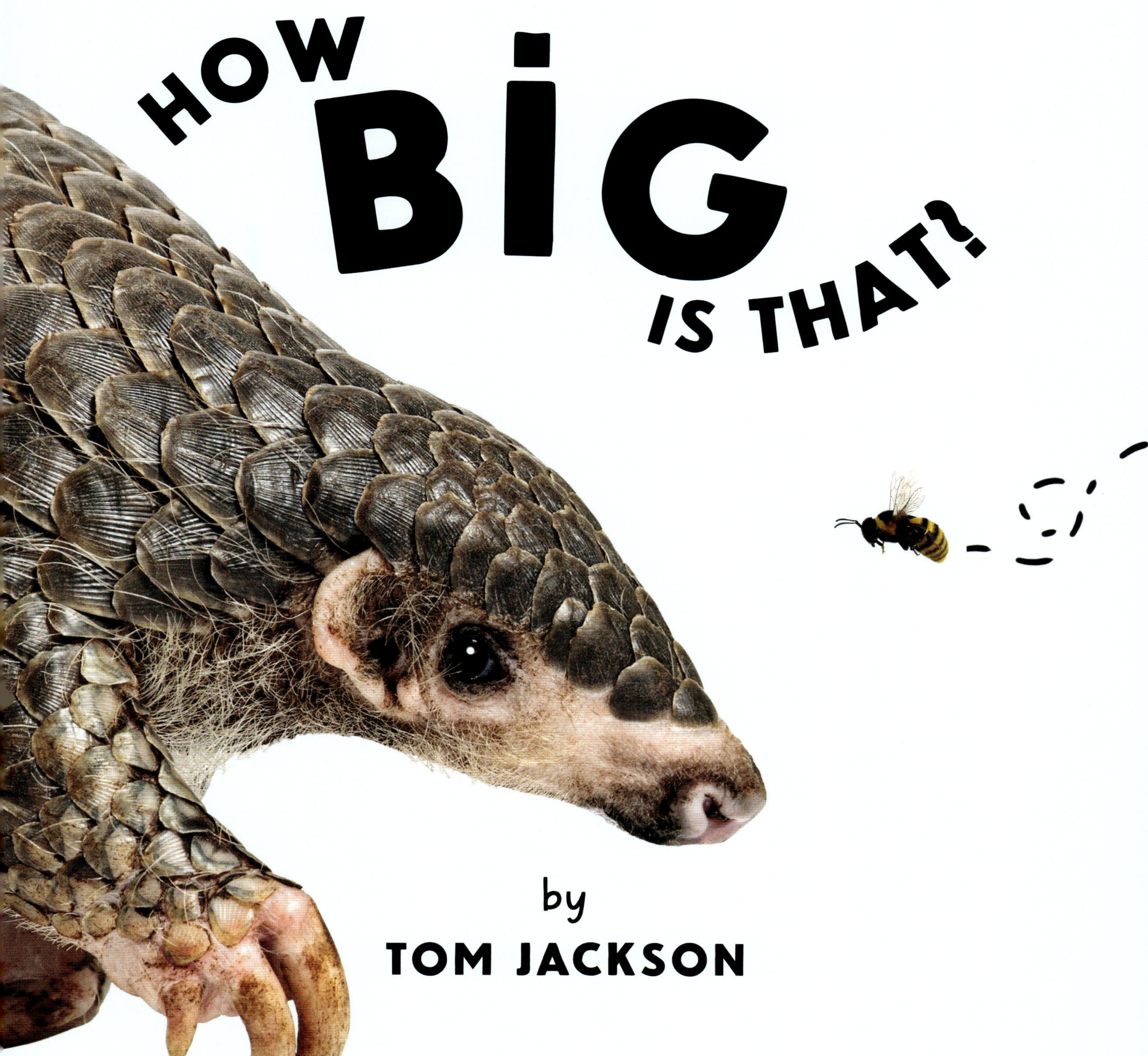

by

TOM JACKSON

An elephant's eyelashes can grow up to **5 inches long**. They protect the eye from dust and sand.

**HAVE YOU EVER BEEN FACE-TO-FACE WITH A FULLY GROWN ELEPHANT? YOU HAVE NOW!**

*Inside this book you will see more than 100 animals as they really are. Get up close to a shark's teeth—that's close enough! See a giraffe's tongue, the world's smallest bird, a transparent frog, and a lizard that squirts blood from its eyes! And look out for the wombat poop! If you've ever asked* **How Big Is That?** *this book is for you!*

# CONTENTS

1 2 3 4 7 8

10 11 12 13 14 15

# WHY THAT SIZE?

**WHY DON'T WE HAVE SPIDERS AS BIG AS AN ELEPHANT SEAL? HERE ARE SEVERAL FACTORS THAT AFFECT HOW BIG AN ANIMAL IS.**

## WEIGHT LIMIT

*Animals that live in water can grow much larger than those that live on land. This elephant seal is 20 times longer than the weasel, and is 35,000 times heavier! The water supports all this extra weight. The seal is too heavy to move far on land, while the weasel can wriggle almost anywhere.*

## MAXIMUM SIZE

Insects, spiders, and other bugs can never grow very big, because they do not breathe in air. Instead, air just wafts into them. If these animals had bigger bodies, this way of taking in air wouldn't be fast enough. Luckily for them, biting spiders, snapping scorpions, and stinging hornets don't need to be big to survive!

## GOING FROM HOT TO COLD

Animals that live in cold places are bigger than their relatives that live in warmer climates. This is because big bodies hold heat better and waste less energy.

The largest kind of penguin is the emperor penguin, which spends winter in Antarctica. It is twice as tall and 20 times heavier than the Galápagos penguin, which lives far away at the Equator.

# MEASURING UP

**THE BEST THING ABOUT ANIMALS IS THAT THEY ARE ALL SO DIFFERENT. BUT THAT MAKES COMPARING THEM TRICKY.**

Scientists that study animals are called zoologists. A big part of their job is measuring animals. Knowing how long, how tall, and how heavy they are is important for understanding how animals survive. Here are some of the ways animals measure up.

## NOSE TO TAIL

This is the maximum length of an animal. A **butterfly fish** has a pointed snout, but a fan-shaped tail!

## NOSE TO RUMP

This is the way to measure the main body of an animal. The **titan beetle** is one of the biggest insects of all.

1 2 3 4 5 6 7 8

## HEAD HEIGHT

A good way to measure a bird is to the top of the head—including this **cardinal's** crest!

## SHOULDER HEIGHT

Four-legged animals, such as this **wood mouse**, are best measured to the shoulder, or the tops of their front legs.

## WINGSPAN

Flying animals like this **monarch butterfly** are often measured by their wingspan, which is the distance between the tips of the wings.

## STRANGE SHAPES

Some animals are much harder to measure. For example, an octopus has no shoulders or tail, but eight arms —and which part is the head?

## ADVANTAGES OF BEING BIG

**BISON**
9 feet

Big bodies are efficient. Large animals use food energy better, so they need to eat less food to stay alive.

**HIPPOPOTAMUS**
16 feet

Giant animals are safe from attack because predators are often too small to hurt them.

**CHEETAH**
5 feet

A big animal is always stronger and faster than a small one—so predators are often big.

## ADVANTAGES OF BEING SMALL

**BUSH BABY**
6 inches

It is easier for small animals to find places to stay out of sight.

**KINGFISHER**
6 inches

Smaller animals only need a small meal of nutritious food to fill them up.

**ANT**
0.2 inches

Small animals are very strong for their size, so can lift objects larger than they are.

11 12 13 14 15 16 17

# MAMMALS

**MAMMALS ARE MOSTLY KIND OF HAIRY. THEY ALSO INCLUDE WHALES, THE LARGEST ANIMALS OF ALL, PLUS MANY THAT ARE MUCH SMALLER!**

When the first scientists saw a **platypus**, with its webbed feet and duck bill, they thought it was a fake!

Like many other mammals that live in the water, the **gray seal** has only short, waterproof hairs. The seal uses the thick whiskers that poke out of its face to pick up currents in the water. It can feel a fish swimming by, even in the middle of the night!

The **capybara** is the world's largest rodent. Other rodents include mice and squirrels, and the capybara is 1,000 times heavier!

The **bumblebee bat** is the shortest mammal of all. It is only 1.1 inches long and weighs just 0.07 ounces.

The platypus's duck bill is an electric scanner that locates shellfish hiding in mud.

The **giraffe** is the world's tallest animal. The tips of its ossicles (horn-like bones on the head) are 18 feet up.

The **Etruscan shrew** is the smallest mammal. It weighs just 0.06 ounces. To stay alive, this tiny fur ball needs to eat twice its weight in food every day!

# ELEPHANT

Elephants have enormous **TOENAILS** that are around 4 inches wide. There are four on the front feet, but only three on the hind feet. The toenails protect the huge feet from sharp stones.

THE AFRICAN BUSH ELEPHANT IS THE LARGEST LAND ANIMAL ON EARTH. IT IS FAMOUS FOR ITS LONG, FLEXIBLE TRUNK, SPIKED TUSKS, AND HUGE EARS.

Elephants use their flat feet to pick up **DEEP SOUNDS** that they send to each other through the ground. You can see when an elephant is listening carefully because it lifts up one of its front feet.

An elephant's **EARS** are not just for hearing. The great, gray flaps are 4 feet wide. They are there to waft away flies and keep the mighty animal cool. The elephant also waves its ears to frighten away threats.

## VITAL STATS

Scientific name .......... **LOXODONTA AFRICANA**

Height .......... **UP TO 13 FT**

Weight .......... **UP TO 15,000 LB**

Length of trunk .......... **UP TO 7 FT**

Each of an elephant's two **TUSKS** is a front tooth that just keeps on growing. It gets 7 inches longer every year and can end up almost 10 feet long!

LISTEN TO THIS! MOST ANIMALS CAN HEAR MUCH BETTER THAN US. JUST TAKE A LOOK AT THE EARS!

# ALL EARS

A **barn owl's** ears are hidden by feathers. One is higher than the other, which helps the bird hear what's above and below.

A **jackrabbit** is known for its big ears. They help the fast-running hare get rid of unwanted body heat.

The tiny ears of a **greater wax moth** are on its belly. When its ears pick up the high-pitched calls of bats, the moth flies in a loop to avoid being eaten.

Crickets are noisy bugs! They listen for each others' loud calls using the ears on their knees.

Hopping along like a tiny kangaroo, the **jerboa**, a desert rat, has the largest ears of any animal compared to its body size. The ears alone make up two fifths of the body length!

The **American bullfrog** has big ears, so it can hear other frogs' booming croaks. The ears have no outer flaps, just a round eardrum on the side of the head, behind the eye.

The little **fennec fox** uses its huge ears to listen out for sounds of lizards and bugs buried in sand—and then pounces!

Compared to the size of its body, the **serval** has the biggest ears of any cat. It can even spin the tall ears to face backward and hear what is going on behind it.

# ON THE TIP OF MY TONGUE

**A TONGUE IS AN IMPORTANT SENSORY ORGAN. IN ANIMALS, IT CAN BE STICKY, SLIMY, SPIKY, OR SUPERSIZED!**

A **giraffe** has a grasping black tongue to grab and tear leaves. It has to be tough, to protect it from the spiky thorns of acacia plants.

Like all snakes, a **python** tastes the air with its tongue to get information about its surroundings. The fork at the end gives the snake an all-round experience, a bit like surround sound on speakers.

Chameleons drink by catching dewdrops from leaves with their tongues!

The sticky pad at the end of a **chameleon's** tongue smashes down, immobilizing its prey before pulling it back into the waiting mouth.

By poking out its bright blue tongue, a **skink** can startle a predator, giving it time to make a quick getaway.

The mouthparts of a **common fly** are a bit like a straw with a sponge attachment. They allow the fly to suck and mop up tasty juices, from the food on your plate to animal poop.

An **anteater's** noodlelike tongue can vacuum up 30,000 tiny ants or termites a day!

Bristles on their tongues made from keratin—the same substance as your hair and nails—help **penguins** to keep hold of slippery fish.

Tiny but mighty tongue muscles allow **hummingbirds** to slurp nectar at high speeds while hovering.

10 11 12 13 14 15 16 17

# BIRDS

**FLYING IS NOT EASY. HAVE YOU EVER TRIED? BIRDS CAN FLY SO WELL THANKS TO THEIR FEATHERED WINGS AND SLEAK BODIES, LARGE AND SMALL!**

The **wandering albatross** has the widest wingspan of any bird. The wings are for soaring over the ocean to look for fish below. Its big webbed feet help it splash down on the surface to feed.

The bird-of-paradise family from New Guinea is famed for bright coloring and long tail feathers. The **king bird-of-paradise** is the smallest species of all.

The **Atlantic puffin** is a little bird that spends weeks hunting for fish out at sea. It uses its wide beak to hold several fish at once. In summer, it will carry these fish to burrows on land to feed its chicks.

Only the male birds-of-paradise are brightly colored. They dance in the treetops for the females.

1 2 3 4 8

The smallest bird of all is the **bee hummingbird**. It flaps its wings more than 100 times a second to hover in the air.

The bee hummingbird can sip nectar from more than 1,000 flowers in a single day!

The **peregrine falcon** is a kind of bird of prey, or raptor. Raptors are birds that grab prey with their powerful, hooked feet.

THIS HUMMINGBIRD HAS THE WORLD'S LONGEST BEAK FOR ITS SIZE. ALL HUMMINGBIRDS ARE RECORD-BREAKERS. THEY FLAP THEIR WINGS SO FAST, THEY APPEAR AS A BLUR!

# SWORD-BILLED HUMMINGBIRD

The **SWORD-BILLED HUMMINGBIRD** *lives in mountain jungles in South America. Like all hummingbirds, it hovers near flowers and uses its beak to reach the nectar inside.*

# ZOOM IN!

Hummingbirds have small triangular wings. They can flap 100 times a second. The fast **WING BEATS** make a **HUMMING NOISE.**

A hummingbird laps **NECTAR** using a long **TONGUE** that pokes out from the tip of the beak. The tube-shaped tongue flicks in and out up to 20 times a second.

The sword-billed hummingbird beak can be more than 4 inches long. No other bird has a beak that is as **LONG** as the **REST OF ITS BODY** like this.

## VITAL STATS

Scientific name .......... **ENSIFERA ENSIFERA**
Head–body length ...................... **5 IN**
Weight ...................... **0.35–0.55 OZ**
Beak length ................ **UP TO 5 IN**

# IN THE BLINK OF AN EYE

EYES ARE THE MOST IMPORTANT SENSE ORGAN FOR MOST ANIMALS. LOOK HERE TO FIND OUT MORE!

The **ostrich** has the biggest eye of any animal that lives on land. It is nearly five times bigger than a human eye—that's about the size of a pool ball.

This **gecko** is named the **tokay** after the sound of its call. It has no eyelids and so licks its eyeballs to keep them nice and clean.

The **wolf spider** will win any staring competition. It has eight eyes arranged in three rows on its head.

The bulging green-blue eyes of this **dragonfly** each have 24,000 lenses in them. This kind of insect eye is called a compound eye, and it's great for spotting moving prey.

Almost all of the dragonfly's head is filled with its eyes. Its brain is only half the size of a grain of rice.

**Tigers**, like all cats, can see in the dark, thanks to a mirror layer behind the eye that captures every beam of light.

A **panther chameleon** is always on the lookout for a tasty insect to gobble up. It can swivel each of its eyes separately. That means it can look in two places at once. Imagine that!

# WHOSE NOSE?

**A NOSE IS MORE THAN A SMELL SENSOR. ANIMALS USE THEIR NOSES FOR SQUIRTING WATER, SENDING SIGNALS, AND EVEN AS AIR FILTERS.**

The **horned anole** is nicknamed the "Pinocchio lizard" because adult males grow a long, pointed snout to attract mates.

"Proboscis" is another word for nose. Can you see how the **proboscis monkey** got its name? The females' noses are more pointy than this male's.

An elephant's trunk has 40,000 muscles in it, while a person has just 600 in their whole body!

Another name for a **sengi** is "elephant shrew." People thought they were a kind of shrew that had a trunk like an elephant. However, sengis are in fact tiny relatives of elephants that just happen to look a bit like shrews!

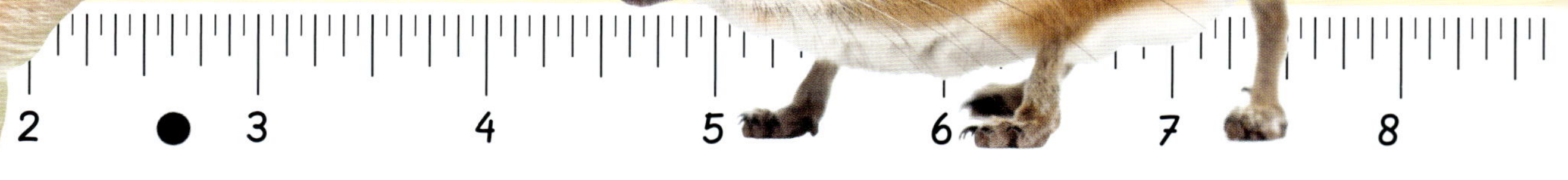

2 3 4 5 6 7 8

The **rhinoceros viper** has spikes on its snout. These "horns" make it harder for prey to spot the snake as it waits among the leaves, ready to strike.

The **saiga antelope** lives in the grasslands of Central Asia, where summers are very dry and dusty. The antelope filters out the dust using sticky skin flaps deep inside its tube-shaped nose.

An **elephant** trunk is the world's largest nose. It sucks up water, trumpets hello, and can also pick things up.

# REPTILES AND AMPHIBIANS

**AMPHIBIANS ARE SLIMY, WHILE REPTILES ARE SCALY, AND THEY INCLUDE EVERYTHING FROM TINY FROGS AND NEWTS TO GIANT TURTLES AND REAL-LIFE DRAGONS!**

The **leatherback turtle** is one of the largest reptiles in the world. Adults are 10 feet long. But they start out small, like these babies that have just hatched from eggs.

The komodo dragon has a slow-acting venom in its spit that weakens and eventually kills its large prey.

A **glass frog** has very thin skin—thin enough for you to see all the way through. Being transparent helps the frog stay hidden among the green forest leaves.

This mini-monster is an **axolotl**—a name that means "monster" in the old Atzec language. These strange newts spend their whole lives in water, breathing with feathery gills. They are only found wild in a few lakes in Mexico City.

1 2 4 5 7 8

The **komodo dragon** is the biggest lizard in the world. It is 10 feet long and attacks wild pigs and buffaloes.

The **green basilisk** is a forest lizard that jumps into water when it is scared—and then runs away. It has wide feet, so it can run across the surface.

# BOA CONSTRICTOR

THIS HUNTER SLITHERS THROUGH THE JUNGLES OF SOUTH AMERICA. IT IS ONE OF THE LARGEST SNAKES IN THE WORLD. IT CAN GROW TO 13 FEET LONG, WHICH IS TWICE AS LONG AS YOUR BED!

**YOUNG** boa constrictors hunt for prey in trees. Older snakes that are too big and heavy to climb, **SLITHER** along the ground in search of prey. Their **MARKINGS** help them to hide in the leaves.

A boa constrictor kills its prey by **SQUEEZING** it so hard with its coiled body that the victim cannot breathe!

Boa constrictors hunt many kinds of **PREY**. They eat wild pigs, rats, monkeys, and birds—whatever they can catch!

Like all snakes, the boa constrictor **SWALLOWS** its food whole. It can open its mouth very wide, and uses dozens of small **HOOKED TEETH** to pull the food into its mouth.

## VITAL STATS

Scientific name .......... **BOA CONSTRICTOR**

Length ...................... **UP TO 13 FT**

Weight ................................ **60 LB**

Lifespan ...................... **30 YEARS**

# PAWS AND CLAWS

**YOU WON'T WANT TO SHAKE HANDS WITH THESE FIERCE CREATURES! THEIR SHARP OR HOOKED CLAWS LOOK TOO SCARY!**

*The* **Canadian lynx** *is an expert hunter during the cold winter. It has wide feet that will not sink into the soft snow, just like a pair of snowshoes.*

*The* **harpy eagle** *of South America is the largest bird of prey in the world. It swoops through the rainforest snatching monkeys from the branches with its hooked claws, or talons. Each toe is as long as a man's finger!*

*The* **three-toed sloth** *likes to hang around—for days on end. It uses its long, hooked claws to cling to high branches.*

A **giant armadillo** uses its 6-inch claws to break apart ant nests and termite mounds to get a tasty snack, and then dig itself a comfortable burrow for a sleep.

The **southern cassowary** from New Guinea cannot fly, but uses its three long claws as running spikes as it charges through the jungle.

Polar bear fur is not white. The hairs are colorless and see-through but look white from the outside.

Never get this close to a **polar bear** foot. This mighty paw can smash through thick sea ice and kill a seal with one swipe. The bear also uses its wide feet as paddles when it goes for a swim. It can swim 200 miles in one go!

**MANY ANIMALS STAY SAFE INSIDE HARD SHELLS, OR WEAR AN ARMOR OF TOUGH, WATERPROOF SCALES.**

# SHELLS AND SCALES

A **milk snake's** skin is made of colorful, overlapping scales. The snake is harmless, but mimicking the stripes of poisonous snakes keeps predators away.

Sea turtles, like this **hawksbill turtle**, have shells made from thick scales, or scutes. The shell covers the back and the belly, and is attached to the reptile's skeleton.

This **hermit crab** does not grow its own hard shell. Instead, it moves into one left behind by another animal, such as a sea snail.

These beautiful **Cuban painted snails** live in trees. The bright colors confuse predators like birds. Can these really be food?

The **nautilus** is a relative of squids and octopuses. It has even more tentacles than they do. But it also has a beautiful spiral shell that is full of gas bubbles so the animal does not sink in the water.

It may look like a scaly lizard, but the pangolin is a **mammal**. There are bristles between its scales.

The **pangolin** is an anteater. It has no teeth and swallows the insects whole. The lining of its stomach has scaly spikes that crush up the food instead.

Ironclad beetles are too hard for predators to chew, yet the insects eat soft foods, like mushrooms and rotting wood.

**Ironclad beetles** are so tough, it is said they can survive being run over by a car. But it is better not to test this fact—just in case!

# FISH

**TIME TO DIVE DOWN UNDER THE WATER TO VISIT THE WORLD OF FISH. CHECK OUT THE FINS, FANGS, AND ... FLASHLIGHTS?**

*You have nothing to fear from an* **epaulette shark***. These small fish spend their nights crawling around on the seabed searching for shellfish to chomp on. They use fleshy tendrils on their lips to feel their way.*

*The* **Valentin's sharpnosed puffer** *wants to be left alone. When it feels like it's under attack, the fish puffs up its body so it looks bigger. This also pushes little poisoned spikes out of the skin! Swim away!*

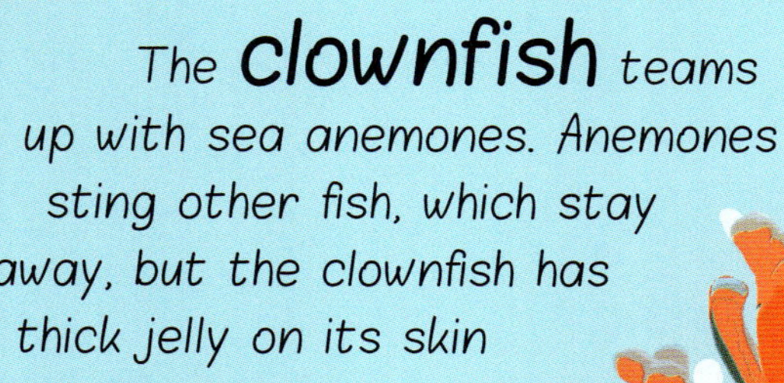

*The* **clownfish** *teams up with sea anemones. Anemones sting other fish, which stay away, but the clownfish has thick jelly on its skin to protect it.*

**Flying fish** leap out of the water to get away from predators. They swish their tails to push themselves up and away, and then glide as far as they can on their stiff fins.

Though it doesn't do much swimming, a **seahorse** is a fish, not a horse. It is usually found hanging on to seaweed with its tail and sucks in tiny bits of food from the water through its tubelike mouth.

Seahorse dads give birth to their babies after keeping the eggs safe in a special pouch on their bellies.

The **flashlight fish** lives deep down in the ocean, where it is dark all the time. However, these fish see using their own light, made by glowing pads under their eyes.

Few fish are as frightening as a **piranha**. They have sharp teeth and a strong bite. When shoals get too crowded, piranhas start to eat their neighbors.

12 13 14 15 16

# GREAT WHITE SHARK

ROWS OF RAZOR-EDGED TEETH, A TOP SPEED OF 35 MILES PER HOUR, AND SUPER-SHARP SENSES MAKE THE GREAT WHITE SHARK A SUPREME HUNTER. IT'S THE WORLD'S LARGEST PREDATORY FISH.

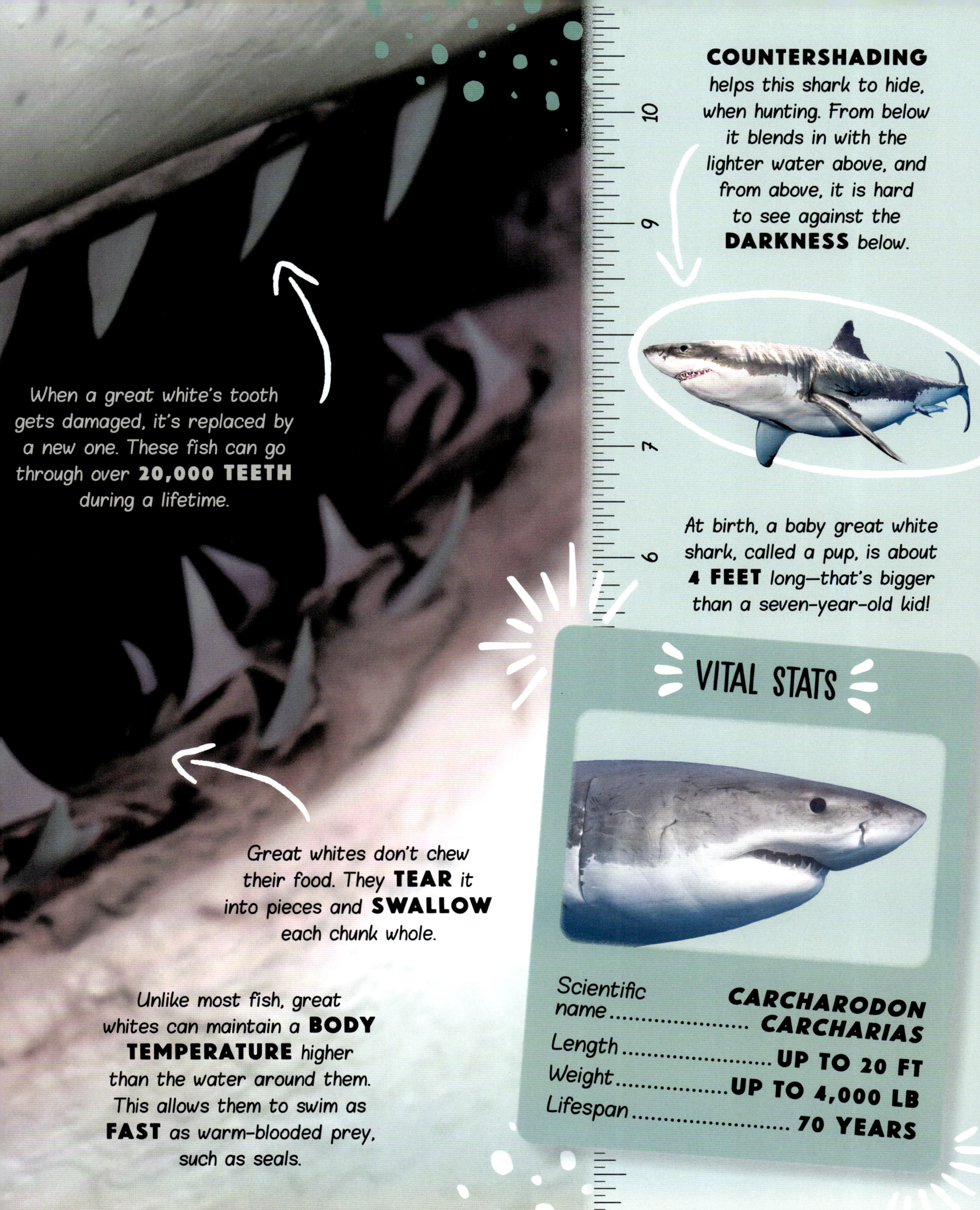

**COUNTERSHADING** helps this shark to hide, when hunting. From below it blends in with the lighter water above, and from above, it is hard to see against the **DARKNESS** below.

When a great white's tooth gets damaged, it's replaced by a new one. These fish can go through over **20,000 TEETH** during a lifetime.

At birth, a baby great white shark, called a pup, is about **4 FEET** long—that's bigger than a seven-year-old kid!

Great whites don't chew their food. They **TEAR** it into pieces and **SWALLOW** each chunk whole.

## VITAL STATS

Scientific name ........................ **CARCHARODON CARCHARIAS**
Length ........................ **UP TO 20 FT**
Weight ................. **UP TO 4,000 LB**
Lifespan ........................ **70 YEARS**

Unlike most fish, great whites can maintain a **BODY TEMPERATURE** higher than the water around them. This allows them to swim as **FAST** as warm-blooded prey, such as seals.

**WATCH OUT! THESE ANIMALS MAY BITE! CHECK OUT SOME OF THE BIGGEST, SHARPEST—AND WEIRDEST—TEETH AROUND.**

The **Sloane's viperfish** is a small deep-sea fish with some very outsize teeth—the largest of any animal compared to its body size. The fish also glows, so those half-inch fangs gleam in the gloom.

# TEETH AND JAWS

A male **narwhal** has only one tooth, but it can be 9 feet long! The long upper tooth pokes out of the whale's top lip, and is sensitive to the saltiness and temperature of the water.

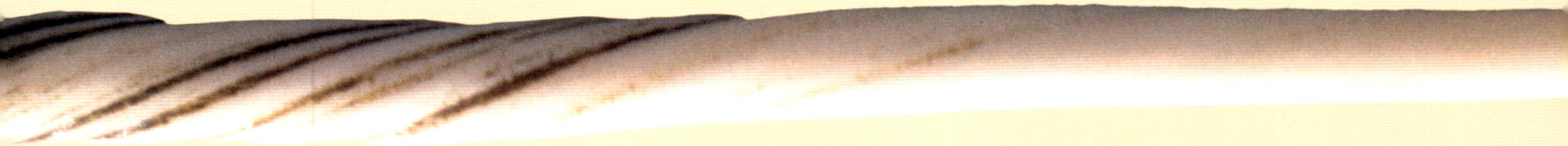

The world's largest reptile, the **saltwater crocodile**, has the strongest bite of any animal. It is four times stronger than a lion's bite, and ten times more powerful than a human's. The giant croc clamps its jaws on prey and drags it under the water.

1 2 3 4

The little hairless **naked mole rat** spends its whole life underground. It digs tunnels through the soil using its long front teeth, searching for roots to eat.

The **babirusa** is a wild pig from Indonesia. Its curved 5-inch tusks are teeth that grow so long that they poke through the hog's skin!

Viking traders used to sell the long, spiraled tusks of narwhals, saying they were actually the horns of unicorns.

**Stag beetles** look like they have horns (or antlers—like real stags). However, they are actually long, pincer-like mouthparts called mandibles.

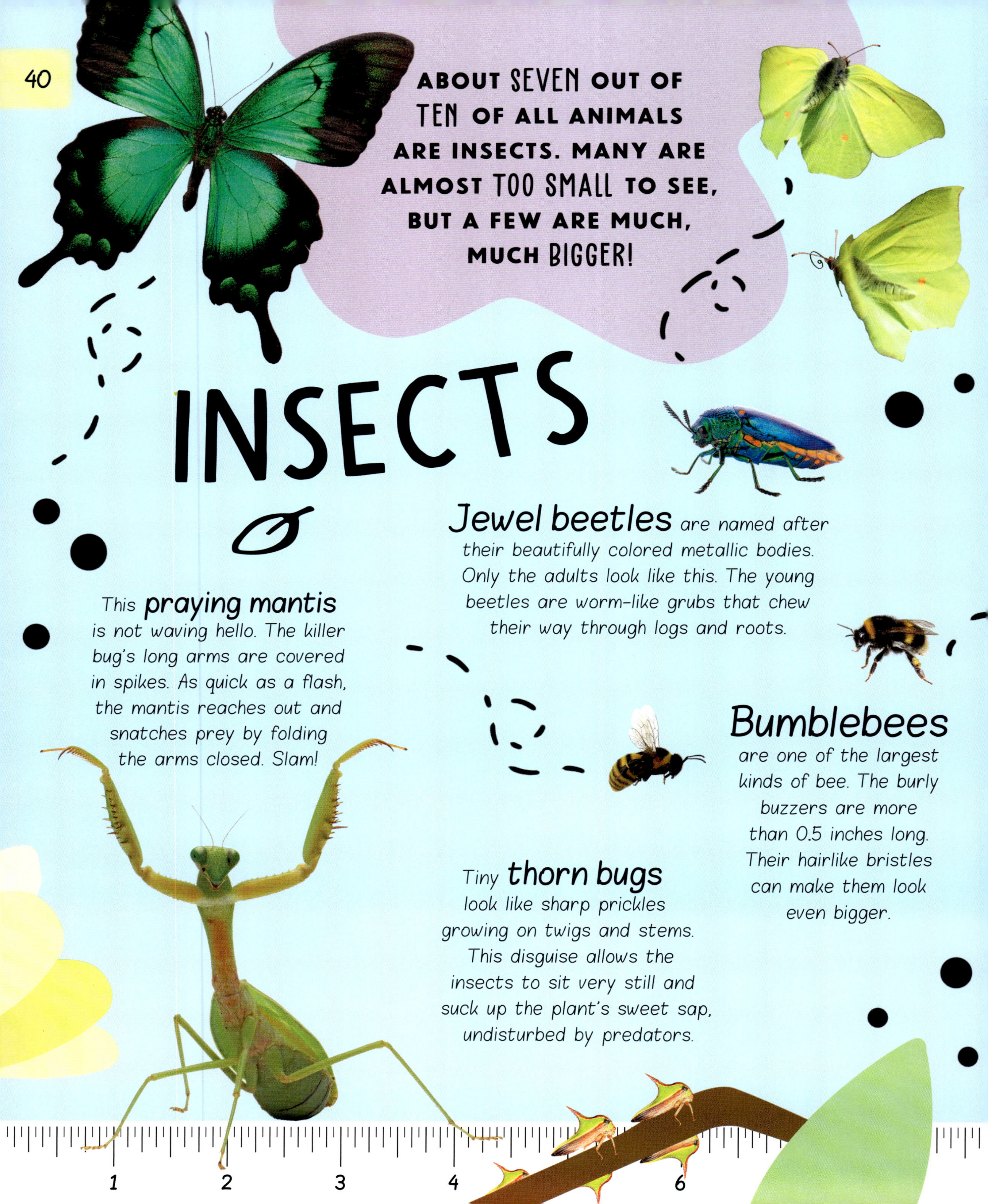

**ABOUT SEVEN OUT OF TEN OF ALL ANIMALS ARE INSECTS. MANY ARE ALMOST TOO SMALL TO SEE, BUT A FEW ARE MUCH, MUCH BIGGER!**

# INSECTS

This **praying mantis** is not waving hello. The killer bug's long arms are covered in spikes. As quick as a flash, the mantis reaches out and snatches prey by folding the arms closed. Slam!

**Jewel beetles** are named after their beautifully colored metallic bodies. Only the adults look like this. The young beetles are worm-like grubs that chew their way through logs and roots.

**Bumblebees** are one of the largest kinds of bee. The burly buzzers are more than 0.5 inches long. Their hairlike bristles can make them look even bigger.

Tiny **thorn bugs** look like sharp prickles growing on twigs and stems. This disguise allows the insects to sit very still and suck up the plant's sweet sap, undisturbed by predators.

The **blue morpho** is a big, beautiful butterfly that lives in the jungles of Central America. Only the top side of the wings are blue, creating flashes of distracting color as the insect flies. When it lands, the morpho folds up its wings to show only the greenish brown undersides.

Despite their name, **fireflies** are actually beetles. And only the males can fly. The females stay as grubs crawling around trees. The beetles find each other using the light from their glowing abdomens.

As its name suggests, the **stalk-eyed fly** has eyes on the ends of long stalks. Instead of fighting for mates, the males measure themselves against each other. The one with the widest eyes wins!

A firefly's glow is made by mixing chemicals together. They give out green, yellow, or red light.

The male **giraffe weevil** has a very long neck, which it uses to impress females. When two males meet, they swing their necks at each other, hoping to knock over their enemy.

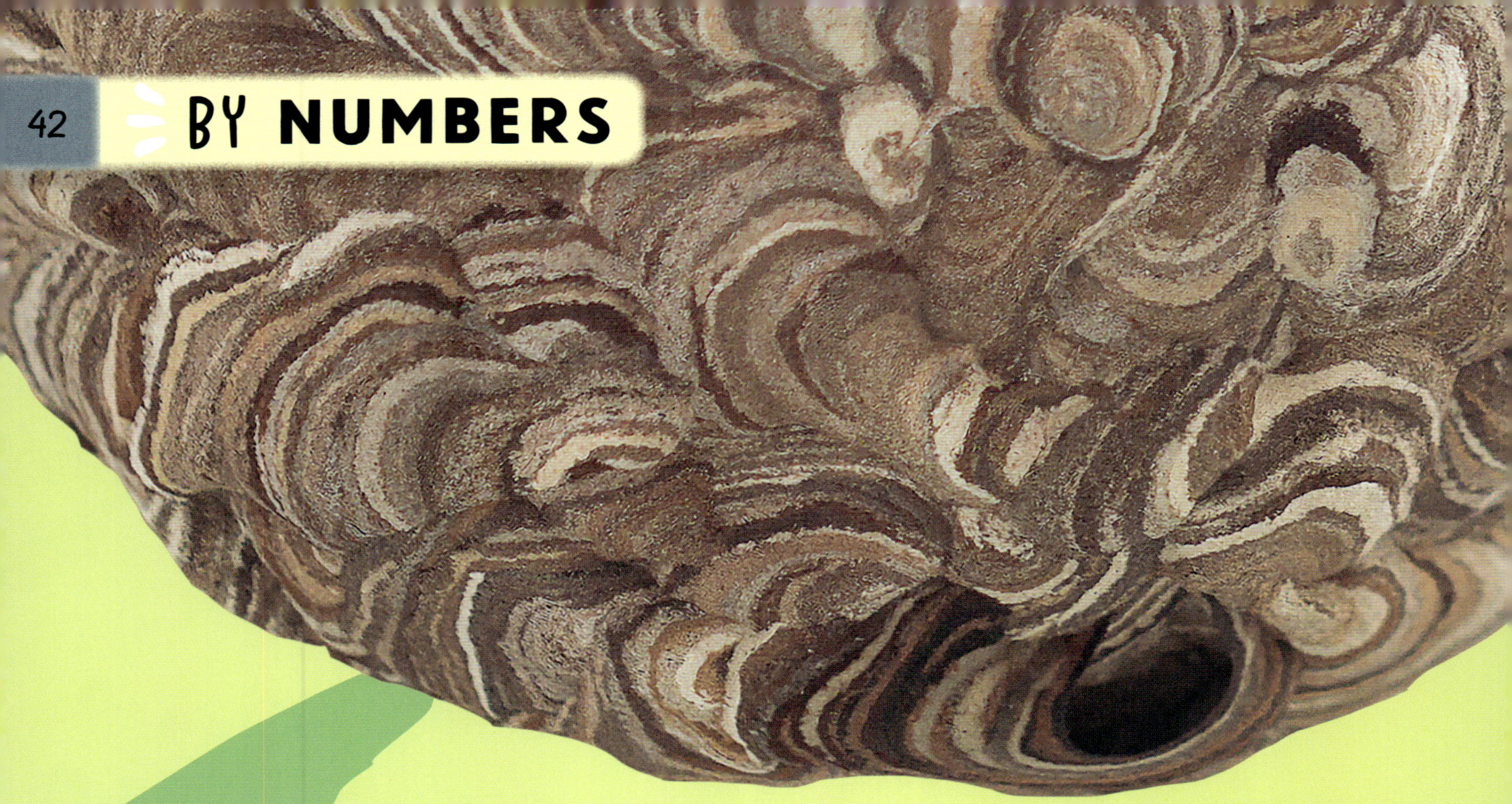

# HORNET

**HORNETS ARE LARGE RELATIVES OF WASPS AND BEES. THEY CAN GIVE PAINFUL STINGS AND ARE TOUGH KILLERS THAT CHOP UP OTHER INSECTS AND FEED THEM TO THEIR YOUNG.**

honey bee

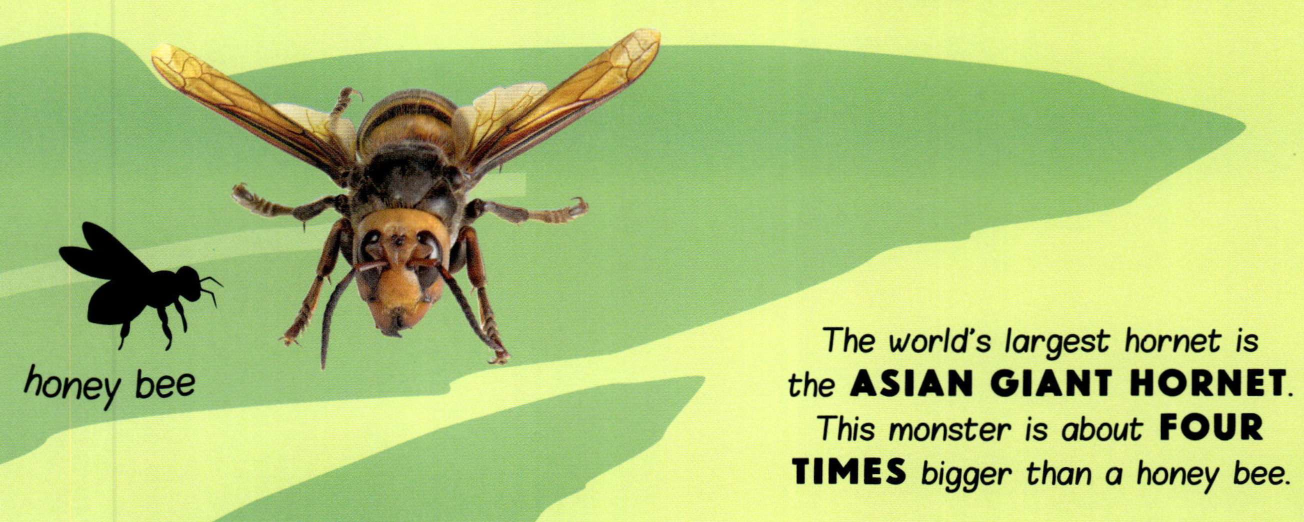

*The world's largest hornet is the* **ASIAN GIANT HORNET**. *This monster is about* **FOUR TIMES** *bigger than a honey bee.*

Hornets live in a group containing around **100 INSECTS**. They work together to build a **PAPER NEST** made from strips of chewed-up wood.

Asian giant hornets come from **EAST ASIA**, including China and Japan. They are most common in **MOUNTAIN FORESTS**. However, these big insects are now spreading around the world.

Giant hornets have a wingspan of 3 inches. There are **FOUR WINGS**. The hind wings are much smaller than the pair in front.

A group, or **COLONY**, of hornets is ruled by a **QUEEN**. The queen is the mother of all the other hornets in the group.

## ZOOM IN!

**ADULT** hornets use their stings to kill other insects. They take them back to the nest as **FOOD** for the young growing inside.

## VITAL STATS

Scientific name........ **VESPA MANDARINIA**

Length........................ **UP TO 2 IN**

Weight.................................. **1 OZ**

Top speed........................ **25 MPH**

UP, UP AND AWAY! WONDERFUL WINGS TAKE FLYING ANIMALS INTO THE AIR. BIG WINGS ARE GOOD FOR GOING HIGH, WHILE SMALL ONES ARE BEST FOR STEERING.

# WONDER WINGS

**Rüppell's vulture** has wings about 8 feet wide. The bird can fly higher than Mount Everest.

This **pipistrelle bat** is one of the world's most common bat species. Bats are mammals—they have hair, not feathers—and fly with wings made of skin stretched over long finger bones!

**Beetles**, like this **scarab**, are the most common type of insect of all. They store their wings under hard covers. The covers fold up when the insect flies.

The **Queen Alexandra's birdwing** has an 11-inch wingspan, the largest of any butterfly (and any insect). This one is a male, and the females are even bigger!

**Gnats** are tiny flies that are almost too small to see. Some bite skin and suck blood, so you might feel them before you see them!

Big birdwing butterflies are very rare because they are taken from the wild by collectors.

The **little owl** is only 9 inches tall. Owl wings are shaped so they make almost no noise as the bird swoops in to kill prey.

# TURNING TAIL

Ring-tailed lemurs use their tails to waft bad smells at their enemies!

**WE HUMANS ARE UNUSUAL ANIMALS: NONE OF US HAVE TAILS! CHECK OUT HOW THESE AMAZING CREATURES USE THEIRS.**

**Ring-tailed lemurs** are relatives of monkeys that live in Madagascar. They hold up their 2-foot black-and-white striped tails so the members of their troop can keep track of each other.

The **Asian grass lizard's** body is 12 inches long, but its slender, whip-like tail is three times longer! If the lizard is attacked, the tail drops off! A new, shorter one grows back.

A tail that wraps around objects is called prehensile. Monkeys with prehensile tails only live in the Americas.

The **woolly spider monkey** is a very rare species from South America. It has the longest tail of any monkey—an adult's tail is about 30 inches long. The tail is used as a third arm for holding branches.

The **peacock** is famous for showing off its fan-shaped tail, which has many colorful eye-spot feathers.

Male **Siamese fighting fish** will attack each other if they get too close. Their long, flowing tail fins swish and swirl in the water.

**INVERTEBRATES ARE ANIMALS WITHOUT A BACKBONE. AS WELL AS INSECTS, THEY INCLUDE A WIDE RANGE OF CREEPY-CRAWLIES, SUCH AS CRABS AND SPIDERS.**

# CREEP AND CRAWL

*Scorpions are relatives of spiders. They have pincers and a sting in the tail. The* **emperor scorpion** *is one of the world's largest, reaching 7 inches long. The sting hurts, but is not dangerous to humans.*

*With its jointed legs and hard shell, the* **red apple crab** *is a type of crustacean. Baby crabs are the size of a pea, while the largest species, the Japanese spider crab, grows as long as a car!*

*Millipede means "one thousand feet," but most of them, including this* **yellow-banded millipede**, *only have around 200. Millipedes live all over the world among rotting leaves. They are related to centipedes, which means "one hundred feet."*

1 2 3 4 5 6 7 8

All spiders are predators. They use fangs to kill prey, and then suck out any meaty juices.

The **goliath birdeater** is a kind of tarantula spider. It has the widest legs and body of any spider and would easily cover a dinner plate. Despite the name, the spider eats worms!

This **red sea star** is typical of a starfish with its five arms. Other starfish can have 50 arms. The animal's mouth is at the center of the star.

**Giant African land snails** are the largest mollusks to live on land. The snail has a tongue-like mouthpart called a radula, which grinds up plant food.

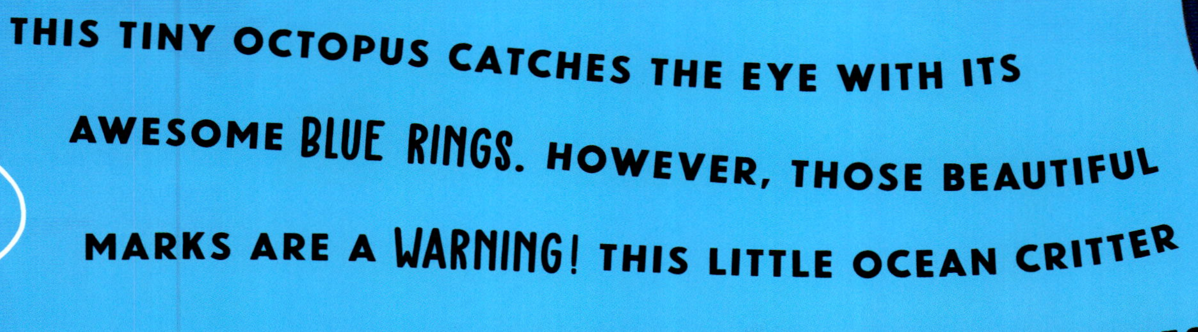

THIS TINY OCTOPUS CATCHES THE EYE WITH ITS AWESOME BLUE RINGS. HOWEVER, THOSE BEAUTIFUL MARKS ARE A WARNING! THIS LITTLE OCEAN CRITTER HAS A DEADLY BITE THAT KILLS IN MINUTES.

# BLUE-RINGED OCTOPUS

*The blue-ringed octopus lives around* **CORAL REEFS** *and in rocky* **TIDE POOLS** *along the coasts of the Indian and Pacific oceans.*

# ZOOM IN!

The blue-ringed octopus has a sharp **BEAK** located at the center of its arms. The beak cuts a hole in prey, and the octopus then spits in some **SALIVA**. The saliva contains a **VENOM** that paralyzes victims.

A bite from this octopus is dangerous, but only about **TEN PEOPLE** are known to have been killed by them.

The little octopus squeezes into the gaps between rocks. It waits for fish or other **PREY** to come near, and then it pounces. The octopus kills its prey with a **VENOMOUS BITE**.

## VITAL STATS

Scientific name .......................... **HAPALOCHLAENA LUNULATA**
Length including arms .............. **6 IN**
Weight .......................................... **2.8 OZ**
Lifespan ..................................... **3 YEARS**

# GROSS OUT

**YUCK! TAKE A LOOK AT SOME OF THE MOST DISGUSTING ANIMALS AROUND. THEY USE SLIME, STINKS, BLOOD, AND EVEN POOP IN UNUSUAL WAYS.**

When a **short-horned lizard** is under attack, it fights back in a disgusting way.

The lizard squirts blood at attackers out of its own eyes!

**Hagfish** are the world's slimiest animals. The slime protects the fish from attack.

The **hairy frog** is named after the male's shaggy skin. When it needs to fight, the bones in the back feet poke out to make claws. It's a bit like a superpower.

**Dung beetles** love dollops of cow poop. They scoop up a ball and roll it to somewhere safe—and then they eat it!

1 3 4 5 6 7

**Skunks** are famous for their terrible stink. If disturbed, they squirt a foul-smelling liquid from their bottoms. If a skunk turns its back on you, it's best to run away!

When a **European roller** chick feels under threat from a predator, it tries to make itself less tasty. The chick is sick on itself, spreading orange vomit (which smells bad) all over its feathers..

Skunk spray smells like burning rubber, rotten eggs, farts, and garlic all at once.

The **wombat** is one of the cutest animals from Australia. This one is a baby, and the adults grow to 40 inches long. Wombats eat grass, and their stomachs make their poop square-shaped!

# BIG AND SMALL BABIES

**AWW... BABY ANIMALS ARE SO CUTE! SOMETIMES LARGE ANIMALS START SMALL, WHILE SMALLER ANIMALS ARE BORN BIG!**

Red kangaroo joey at 6 months

**Red kangaroos** are the largest wild animals in Australia. However, at birth, baby kangaroos, or joeys, are less than 1 inch long—the size of a jellybean. It takes six months to reach the size shown here, and the adults are 6 feet tall.

Size of joey at birth

A tiny, newborn joey crawls through its mom's fur to get to her pouch, where it will grow much larger!

Adults of the **Nile crocodile**, a huge African reptile, are 16 feet long. They all start out as a tiny baby hatching from an egg that is only 2 inches across.

A **pygmy blue whale** calf is already 19 feet long when it is born. Its tail is 4 feet wide.

Adult **silvered leaf monkeys** have gray fur. However, the tiny babies have golden hair. The bright fur is a sign to older monkeys that these little ones need looking after.

The **kiwi** bird lays one egg that is about a third as large as the adult. After hatching, the chick is strong enough to feed itself, digging for worms with its long beak.

The **peacock butterfly** starts as a caterpillar that hatches from an egg the size of a pencil tip. After growing to 1.5 inches long, the caterpillar becomes a pupa, and then a winged adult.

**SOME ANIMALS ARE VERY DANGEROUS, AND THESE DEADLY CREATURES ARE NOT ALWAYS GIANT MONSTERS—BUT OF COURSE SOME OF THEM ARE!**

# WATCH OUT

**Mosquitoes** are tiny flies, less than half an inch long, that suck the blood from larger animals. Many spread diseases, including malaria. This terrible illness kills more than half a million people every year.

**Cone snails** live in warm, shallow seas. They harpoon fish and other prey with their pointy tongues and pump in a poison, or venom. A cone snail's venom is the strongest of any animal. It could kill a person in 30 minutes!

Getting its name from the square shape of its body, the Indian Ocean's **box jellyfish** is small, but its stings can kill a person. The box body is 6 inches wide, but poisoned, stinging tentacles trail out 10 feet behind.

1 2 3 4 5 7 8

When it stands up on its back legs, a **grizzly bear** is 10 feet tall! The bear eats all kinds of foods, such as fish, mushrooms, or deer. Each of its hooked claws is 4 inches long. The bear can kill with a single slap of its mighty paw.

The bear also uses its long claws for digging a cozy den to sleep in during the cold winter.

The **golden poison dart frog** is small enough to sit on your fingertip—but do not let it! Its skin is filled with poison. Forest people from Central America use the poisons in the skin to make hunting darts that kill prey in seconds.

A **deathstalker scorpion** is only about 3 inches long. It lives in the deserts of the Middle East, where it lies in wait for insect prey. If a person picks up this scorpion it will sting. Those attacks are very painful but rarely deadly.

The **saw-scaled viper** is small, but still a big killer. The Asian snake is only 2 feet long, but it bites people a lot and kills thousands every year.

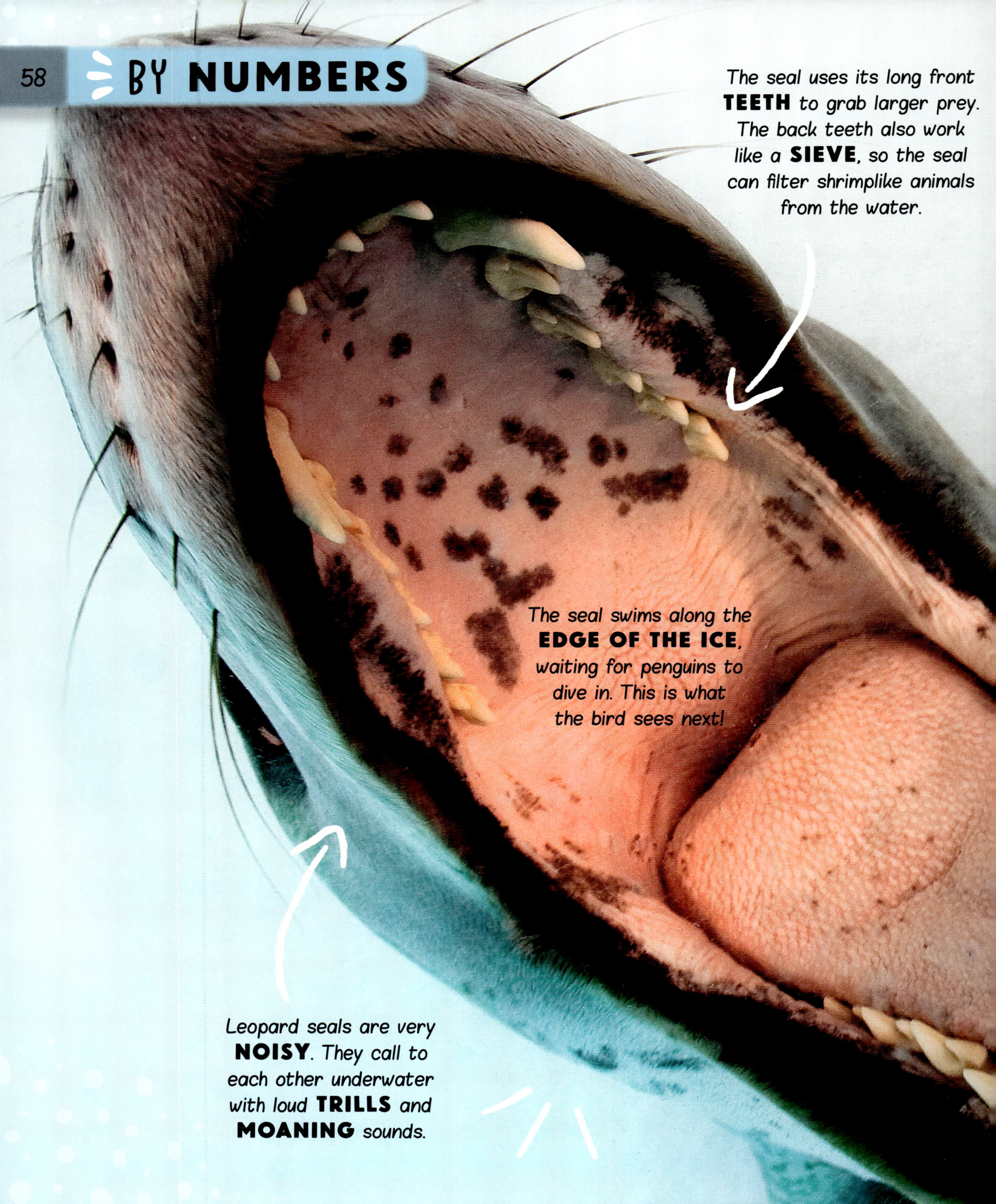

The seal uses its long front **TEETH** to grab larger prey. The back teeth also work like a **SIEVE**, so the seal can filter shrimplike animals from the water.

The seal swims along the **EDGE OF THE ICE**, waiting for penguins to dive in. This is what the bird sees next!

Leopard seals are very **NOISY**. They call to each other underwater with loud **TRILLS** and **MOANING** sounds.

# LEOPARD SEAL

**THIS FIERCE HUNTER SWIMS THROUGH THE COLD OCEANS AROUND ANTARCTICA. IT SEARCHES FOR SQUID OR FISH AND ALSO LOVES TO CHOMP ON PENGUINS!**

The leopard seal is named after the **DARK SPOTS** on its body. It is one of the world's largest seals and is almost twice as long as an adult human.

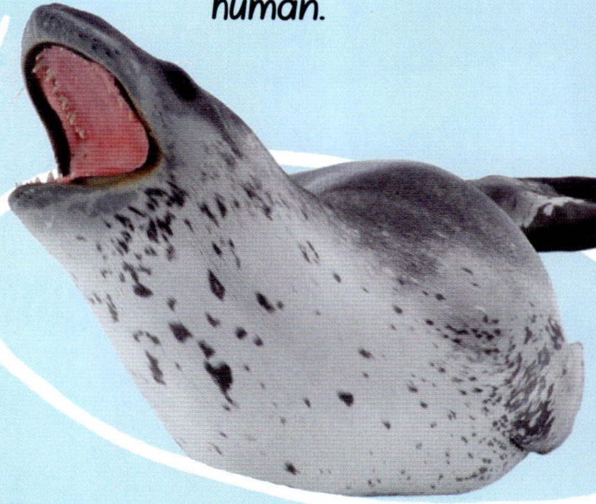

The leopard seal almost never comes out onto land. Instead, it takes a rest on **FLOATING ICE**.

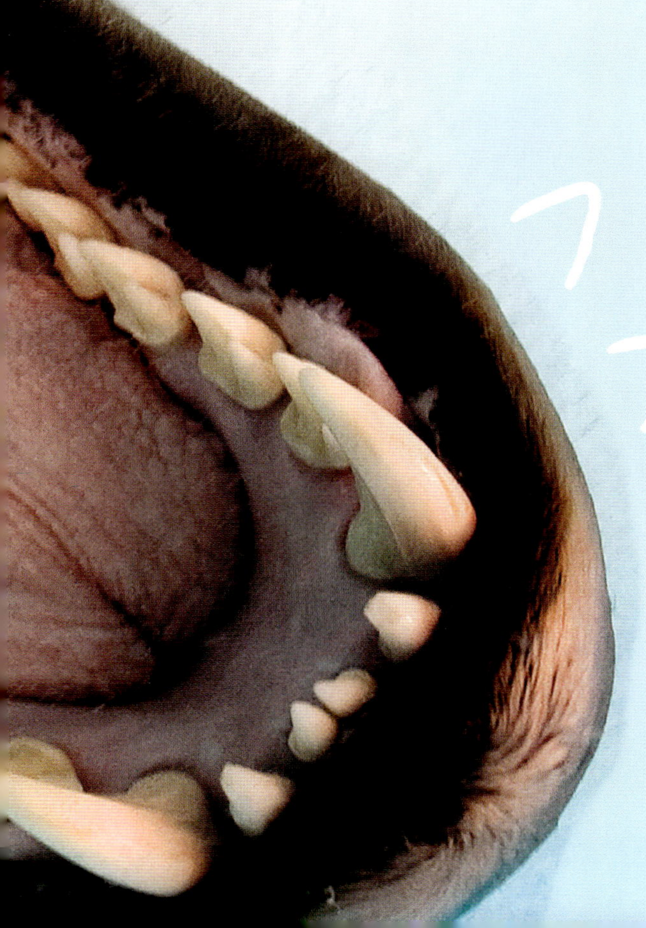

## VITAL STATS

| | |
|---|---|
| Scientific name | **HYDRURGA LEPTONYX** |
| Length | **UP TO 11 FT** |
| Weight | **UP TO 1,300 LB** |
| Lifespan | **15 YEARS** |

# TO SCALE

LET'S SEE SOME ANIMALS STANDING SIDE BY SIDE. THEY HAVE BEEN SHRUNK DOWN ABOUT 25 TIMES TO FIT ON THESE TWO PAGES.

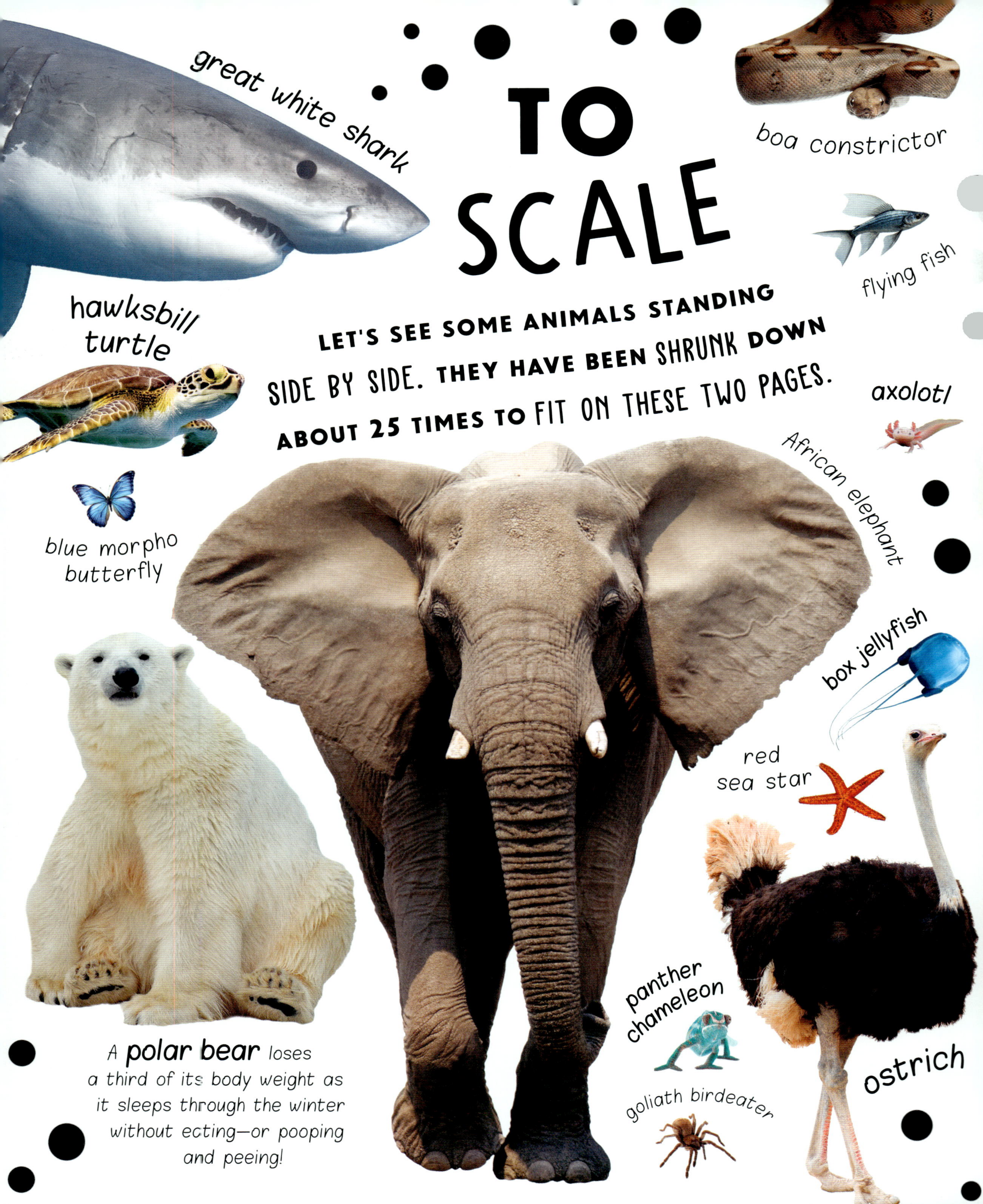


A **polar bear** loses a third of its body weight as it sleeps through the winter without ecting—or pooping and peeing!

Asian grass lizard
pipistrelle bat
grizzly bear
A giraffe only sleeps for 40 minutes a night. It takes too long for it to lie down!
Canadian lynx
peacock
nautilus
fennec fox
little owl
Before using its stinky spray, a skunk will first growl and spit at you, while fluffing up its fur and shaking its tail. Take the hint!
skunk
ring-tailed lemur
Queen Alexandra's birdwing
emperor scorpion
pangolin
The Asian giant hornet is the most dangerous wild animal in Japan. More people die there from reacting to stings than are killed by bears.
giant African landsnail
milk snake
leopard seal

# INDEX

10 11 12 13 14 15 16

Library of Congress Cataloging-in-Publication Data available
ISBN 979-8-225-05614-8

Written by Tom Jackson
Design concept by Ashtyn Botterill
Book design by Sidonie Beresford-Browne at Raspberry Books
Edited by Raspberry Books and Rosie Neave

First published in North America in 2026 by Magic Cat Publishing, an imprint of Lucky Cat Publishing Ltd, Unit 2, Empress Works, 24 Grove Passage, London E2 9FQ, UK



Printed in China 127
First edition, January 2026

10 9 8 7 6 5 4 3 2 1 26 27 28 29 30

# ACKNOWLEDGMENTS

**COVER** (front) mathiasalvez/Adobe Stock; (back, clockwise from top) mathiasalvez/Shutterstock, Danny Ye/Shutterstock, Eric Isselee/Shutterstock, asawinimages/Shutterstock, bluehand/Shutterstock, Wang LiQiang/Shutterstock

**INTERIORS** ***Alamy Stock Photo*** 18 (tc) kristianbell/RooM the Agency; 35 (c) David Fleetham; 52 (c) Brandon Cole Marine Photography; 53 (bl) Gerry Pearce; 55 (tl) Louise Heusinkveld; 58 (m) Steve Jones ***Yushi Osawa*** 11 ***Nature Picture Library*** 10–11 (tc) Joel Sartore/Photo Ark; 31 (tl) Joel Sartore/Photo Ark; 38 (lc) Bryan and Cherry Alexander; 44 (l) Denis-Huot; 54 (bl) Tony Wu ***Shutterstock*** 1 (l) and 33 (r) and 61 Eric Isselee, (r) Art Victoria; 2–3 Brock Loeven; 4 (tl) Dirk Ercken, 4 (cr) Lightspring, (bl) Lauren Suryanata, (br) Duncan JM Fraser; 5 (tc) inhauscreative, (br) and 61 Eric Isselee; 6 (bl) David Osborn, br Toni Genes, (bl) Maridav; 7 (tr) Sebastian Janicki, (tl) Tran The Ngoc, br Polarman; 8 (c) Johannes Kornelius, (bl) Margus Vilbas; 9 (tc) Bonnie Taylor Barry, (tl) Maximillian cabinet, (bc) Lightspring, (bl) Oleg7799, (icons t to b) Mithi Creation, MarbleDesign, bigkai, Rosa Jay, Rudmer Zwerver, Bigzumi; 10 (cl) Passakorn Umpornmaha, (shrimp) TH Media, (bl) Lynn Batchelor-Browning; 11 (bl) Wirestock Creators, (br) Vaclav Volrab; 12 (m) Baehaki Hariri; 13 (cr) and 60 Vibe Images, (br) mapman; 14 (br) Eric Isselee, (tl) Eric Isselee; 15 (cl) yhelfman, (tr) Lauren Suryanata, (bl) Anna Averianova, (bl) Nynke van Holten, (tr) Yerbolat Shadrakhov, (foliage) I am Irix, (flies) I am Irix; 16 (tl) Mary Lane, (cl) Zety Akhzar, (br) and 64 languste; 16–17 (flies and ants) NotionFic; 17 (tl) Paul Looyen, (cr) gan chaonan, (br) edu_photographer_arg; 18 (br) Duncan JM Fraser, (bc) Tony Tilford, (cr) Potapov Alexander, (r) Sumuditha2006; 19 (cl) Wang LiQiang, (c) alle; 20 (c) FotoRequest; 20–21 (bg sky) chainarong06, (b) Rosalie Kreulen, (bg flowers) Rivabegum; 21 (tr) Wang LiQiang, (br) Rajh.Photography; 22 (tc) Eric Isselee, (bl) lessysebastian, (br) Rob Hainer; 23 (bc) and 60 Vladimir Hodac, (tl) Darkdiamond67, (r) Eric Isselee; 24 (bl) Milan Zygmunt, (br) Eric Isselee, (tl) Rosa Jay; 25 (b) Anton_Ivanov, (tl) Scott Delony, (tr) Yakov Oskanov; 26 (bl) and 60 axolotlowner, (c) Kurit afshen; 26–27 (tr) and (tl) Muhammad Iqbal; 27 (br) asawinimages, (tr) Mike Workman; 28–29 and 60 (m) Eric Isselee; 29 (br) Nynke van Holten, (tr) jtmake; 30 (l) Grindstone Media Group, (br) Damsea; 31 (tr) Fazwick; 32 (lc) and 60 Ed Jenkins, (tr) and 61 Nynke van Holten, (t l–r) and 62 Mark Brandon; 33 (bl) GypsyPictureShow, (tl) and 61 DiveIvanov; 34 (c) orlandin, (bl) jindrich_pavelka; 34–35 (cb) mc_pongsatorn, (c) Anastasia Mangindaan; 34–35 (ct) and 60 bilalwebdesigner; 35 (br) Grigorii Pisotsckii, 35 (c) Arunee Rodloy; 37 (tr) Konstantin39, (br) VisionDive; 38 (tr) Diego Grandi; 38–39 (b) Danny Ye; 39 (r) FTG Indonesia, (tl) Eric Isselee, (br) Dejan82; 40 (t) and 60 Abrar Shadid, (bc) Salparadis, (bl) Kurit afshen, (cr) panor156, (cr) Art Victoria, (cr) unpict, (tl) Sailorr, (tr) Andreas von Mallinckrodt; 41 (bl) Hhelene, (cr) SARIN KUNTHONG, (br) khlungcenter; 43 (bl) Wirestock Creators, (c) and 61 Contrail, (br) AyhanTuranMenekay, (tr) David Carillet; 44 (flies) Bahruz Rzayev, (cr) and 61 Rudmer Zwerver, (br) bluehand; 45 (tr) and 61 funny face, (br) and 61 Albert Beukhof; 46 (bl) and 61 dwi putra stock, (c) Eric Isselee, (br) tratong; 47 (tl) and 61 Mrs_ya, (l) Rob Jansen, (br) songpon pengnok, (br) CW-Chill Out; 48 (tc) Eric Isselee, (br) and 63 DAVID RICO, (bl) Kurit afshen, (tr) and 60 Cloudpost; 49 (tr) and 60 fivespots, (bc) and 61 olegius; 50 (bc) QJ Kang; 50–51 (bg) Allexxandar; 51 (bl) Thierry Eidenweil, (br) Thierry Eidenweil, (tl) YUSRAN ABDUL RAHMAN, (tr) Thierry Eidenweil; 52 (tr) PetlinDmitry, (br) Henk Bogaard, (bl) reptiles4all, (t bg) Vectonessa; 53 (r) and 61 Nynke van Holten, (tl) Mikhail Gnatkovskiy; 54 (tr) LifetimeStock, (cr) Jonathan Oberholster; 55 (cr) David Pineda Svenske, (br) Adwo, (c) K.-U. Haessler, (bl) Eric Isselee; 56 (tl) F.Neidl, (tr) Pisut chounyoo, (tr) Kwangmoozaa, (r) and 60 Henryp982; 57 (cl) Dirk Ercken, (bl) Protasov AN, (br) reptiles4all; 58 (tr) Tarpan; 59 (br) and 61 Jan Martin Will; 60 (bl) evaurban (br) Krakenimages.com; 61 (c) Trixy Gatto, (tc) Geoffrey Kuchera, (tr bear) notsuperstar